Math
ADVANTAGE

Teacher's Edition

W9-AUF-252

Georgia Test Preparation

CRCT and Stanford 9

Includes Test Taking Tips and math assessment items for
- multiple choice format
- short answer
- extended response

Grade 1

Harcourt Brace & Company

Orlando • Atlanta • Austin • Boston • San Francisco • Chicago • Dallas • New York • Toronto • London
http://www.hbschool.com

CONTENTS

Scoring Short Answer Responses

Students can use 3-5 minutes to respond to short-answer test questions. Short-Answer Responses are scored using a rubric. Students can receive partial credit for a partially completed or partially correct answer.

Poor sentence structure, word choice, usage, grammar, and spelling does not affect the scoring of short-answer items, unless communication of ideas is impossible to determine.

Scoring Rubric

Response Level	Criteria
Score 2	**Generally accurate, complete, and clear** ____ All of the parts of the task are successfully completed. ____ There is evidence of clear understanding of key concepts and procedures. ____ Student work shows correct set up and accurate computation.
Score 1	**Partially accurate** ____ Some parts of the task are successfully completed; other parts are attempted and their intents addressed, but they are not completed. ____ Answers for some parts are correct, but partially correct or incorrect for others.
Score 0	**Not accurate, complete, and clear** ____ No part of the task is completed with any success. ____ There is little, if any, evidence that the student understands key concepts and procedures.

Help Students Understand What Scorers Expect

1. Discuss the rubric with students.
2. Have students score their own answer to a practice task, using the rubric.
3. Discuss results. Have students revise their work to improve their scores.

Help students develop proficiency with short-answer questions.

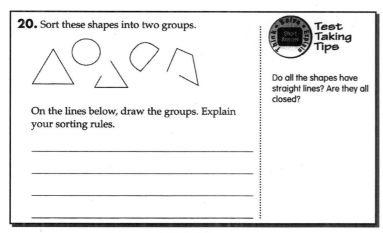

20. Sort these shapes into two groups.

On the lines below, draw the groups. Explain your sorting rules.

Test Taking Tips

Do all the shapes have straight lines? Are they all closed?

Grade 5

Troubleshooting
Use this discussion to help students answer test items effectively.

"I don't get it!"
Help students read the problem carefully. Then ask, "What do you think you are asked to do?"

"What should I write?"
Have students tell you how they solved the problem. Then have them write their words or use pictures.

"Is this the right answer?"
Have students explain how they know that they have answered the question completely.

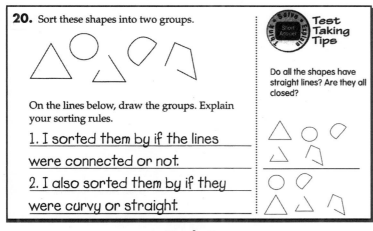

20. Sort these shapes into two groups.

On the lines below, draw the groups. Explain your sorting rules.

1. I sorted them by if the lines were connected or not.
2. I also sorted them by if they were curvy or straight.

Test Taking Tips

Do all the shapes have straight lines? Are they all closed?

Grade 5

Exemplary response
This student has carefully read the problem. She has shown two sorting rules. She has given a thoughtful explanation.

You may want to make a transparency of this example to share with your students.

Have your students evaluate this response to understand why it is clear and complete.

Choose the correct answer.

1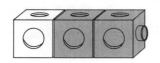

$1 + 2 =$ _____

Ⓐ 3
Ⓑ 4
Ⓒ 5
Ⓓ NOT HERE

2

3 frogs jump.
1 frog sits.
How many in all?

Ⓕ 2 frogs   Ⓗ 4 frogs
Ⓖ 3 frogs   Ⓙ 5 frogs

3

$4 + 1 =$ _____

Ⓐ 3   Ⓒ 5
Ⓑ 4   Ⓓ NOT HERE

4

$4 + 2 =$ _____

Ⓕ 3   Ⓗ 5
Ⓖ 4   Ⓙ NOT HERE

5 Which addition sentence tells how many in all?

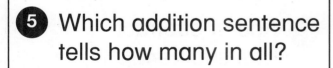

Ⓐ $2 + 1 = 3$
Ⓑ $3 + 1 = 4$
Ⓒ $4 + 1 = 5$
Ⓓ $5 + 1 = 6$

6 Which addition sentence tells how many in all?

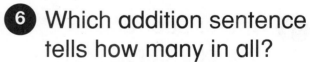

Ⓕ $4 + 2 = 6$
Ⓖ $3 + 2 = 5$
Ⓗ $2 + 2 = 4$
Ⓙ $1 + 2 = 3$

7

4 pups play.
1 walks away.
How many are left?

(A) 1 pup (C) 3 pups
(B) 2 pups (D) 4 pups

8

6 birds eat.
3 fly away.
How many are left?

(F) 2 birds (H) 4 birds
(G) 3 birds (J) 6 birds

9 Which subtraction sentence shows how many are left?

(A) $6 - 3 = 3$ (C) $5 - 1 = 4$
(B) $5 - 2 = 3$ (D) $4 - 0 = 4$

10 Which subtraction sentence shows how many are left?

(F) $6 - 1 = 5$ (H) $6 - 3 = 3$
(G) $6 - 2 = 4$ (J) $6 - 4 = 2$

11 Add or subtract. Use counters.

2 fish swim.
2 more come.
How many in all?

(A) 2 fish (C) 4 fish
(B) 3 fish (D) 5 fish

12 Add or subtract. Use counters.

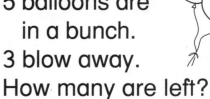

5 balloons are in a bunch.
3 blow away.
How many are left?

(F) 2 balloons (H) 4 balloons
(G) 3 balloons (J) 5 balloons

13 Draw 1 more.
Write the sum.

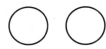

3 + 1 = ____

....

14 How many in all?
Write the sum.

4 + 2 = ____

....

15 My domino has 2 dots on each side. How many dots in all?
Draw the story. Write the addition sentence.

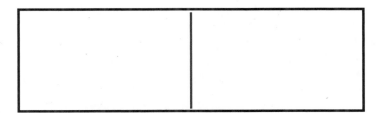

____ + ____ = ____

GO ON

16 Cross out 1.
Write how many are left.

4 – 1 = ___

17 Cross out 2.
Write the difference.

6 – 2 = ___

18 Write the subtraction sentence.

___ – ___ = ___

GO ON

19 Write the difference.

| 5 | – | 1 | = | |

....

20 Add or subtract.

Use counters.

Draw the counters.

6 trucks park.

1 truck goes.

How many trucks are left?

_____ trucks

STOP

Math Advantage Georgia Test Prep   5

Name _____

Choose the correct answer.

1

$$4 + 5 = \underline{\qquad}$$

Ⓐ 6 Ⓒ 8
Ⓑ 7 Ⓓ 9

2 Find the missing sum.

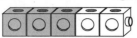

$$3 + 2 = 5$$

$$2 + 3 = \underline{\qquad}$$

Ⓕ 5 Ⓗ 7
Ⓖ 6 Ⓙ 8

3 Use counters.

Which is a way to make 8?

Ⓐ 2 + 4 Ⓒ 5 + 2
Ⓑ 5 + 3 Ⓓ 7 + 2

4 Count on to add.

$$8 + 1 = \underline{\qquad}$$

Ⓕ 6 Ⓗ 9
Ⓖ 8 Ⓙ 10

5

Kim has 6 berries.
Mom gives her 3 more.
How many berries
does Kim have now?

Ⓐ 3 Ⓒ 9
Ⓑ 6 Ⓓ 10

6 Find the doubles fact that goes with the picture.

Ⓕ 2 + 2 = 4
Ⓖ 3 + 3 = 6
Ⓗ 4 + 4 = 8
Ⓙ NOT HERE

GO ON

7

6 frogs are on a log.
2 jump off.
How many frogs now?

Ⓐ 2 frogs   Ⓒ 4 frogs
Ⓑ 3 frogs   Ⓓ NOT HERE

8 $6 + 3 = 9$
$3 + 6 = 9$
$9 - 3 = 6$
$9 - 6 =$ _____

Ⓕ 2   Ⓗ 4
Ⓖ 3   Ⓙ 5

9

$$\begin{array}{r} 5 \\ +0 \\ \hline \end{array}$$

Ⓐ 5   Ⓒ 7
Ⓑ 6   Ⓓ 8

10

$$\begin{array}{r} 4 \\ -0 \\ \hline \end{array}$$

Ⓕ 0   Ⓗ 3
Ⓖ 2   Ⓙ 4

11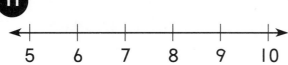

$9 - 3 =$ _____

Ⓐ 5   Ⓒ 7
Ⓑ 6   Ⓓ 8

12

$$\begin{array}{r} 7 \\ -5 \\ \hline \end{array}$$

Ⓕ 0   Ⓗ 2
Ⓖ 1   Ⓙ 3

GO ON

13 Color ⬭ to show one way to make 7.
Write the number sentence.

◯ ◯ ◯ ◯ ◯ ◯ ◯

____ + ____ = ____

....

14 Toss 10 two-color counters.

Write how many red and how many yellow for each toss.

How many different ways can you make 10?

....

15 Write the sums. Circle the one with doubles.

$$\begin{array}{r} 5 \\ + 5 \\ \hline \end{array}$$

$$\begin{array}{r} 4 \\ + 3 \\ \hline \end{array}$$

16 Draw a picture to solve.

6 blue flowers grow.

3 red flowers grow.

How many flowers grow in all? _____ flowers

· ·

17 Use counters.
Solve.

· ·

18 Use 10 counters. Show a fact family.

Draw a picture.

Write two number sentences.

____ + ____ = ____

____ + ____ = ____

GO ON

Name _____

19 Use the number line.
Count back to subtract.

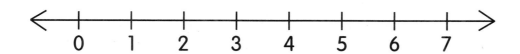

$7 - 3 =$ ___

....

20

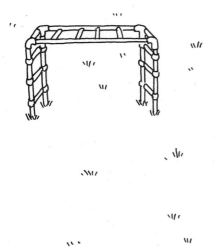

Draw to solve.

Ashley is at the park.

Six girls come.

How many girls are there in all?   ___ girls

Did you use addition or subtraction? _____

© Harcourt

Math Advantage Georgia Test Prep   11

STOP

Choose the correct answer.

1 What is the name of this plane figure?

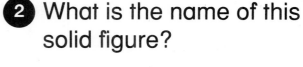

Ⓐ rectangle Ⓒ square
Ⓑ circle Ⓓ triangle

2 What is the name of this solid figure?

Ⓕ sphere Ⓗ cube
Ⓖ cone Ⓙ NOT HERE

3 Which figure has 4 sides and 4 corners?

Ⓐ △

Ⓒ ▢

Ⓑ ⬠

Ⓓ ◯

4 Which plane figure has the same shape?

Ⓕ ▢

Ⓗ ▭

Ⓖ ◯

Ⓙ △

5 Which shape is **larger than** this one?

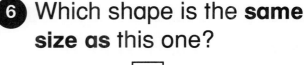

Ⓐ ◯ Ⓑ ◯

6 Which shape is the **same size as** this one?

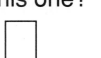

Ⓕ ▭ Ⓖ ▭

GO ON

Name _____

Use the grid for questions
7 and 8.

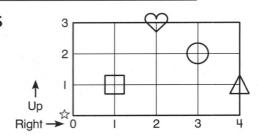

---

7 Start at ☆. Go right 3.
Go up 2. Which shape
is there?

Ⓐ ◯   Ⓒ △

Ⓑ ♡   Ⓓ ☐

8 Start at ☆. Go right 4.
Go up 1. Which shape
is there?

Ⓕ ◯   Ⓗ △

Ⓖ ♡   Ⓙ ☐

---

9 Which line makes two
sides that match?

 Ⓐ   Ⓒ

 Ⓑ   Ⓓ

10 Which picture shows the
bird **inside** the cage?

Ⓕ

Ⓖ

---

11 Which is next in the
pattern?

 Ⓐ   Ⓒ

 Ⓑ   Ⓓ

12 What number is next in
the pattern?

2, 4, 6, 8, 10, ___

Ⓕ 8   Ⓗ 12

Ⓖ 10   Ⓙ 14

GO ON ▶

Name _____

13 Circle the ones you can stack.

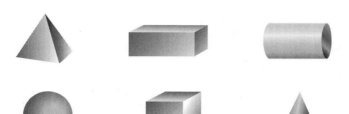

....

14 Circle the shapes with a round face.

....

15 What shape could you trace from each?
Draw each shape below.

Idea Bank
square
triangle
rectangle

Math Advantage Georgia Test Prep   15

© Harcourt

Name _____

16 Make a figure the same size and shape.

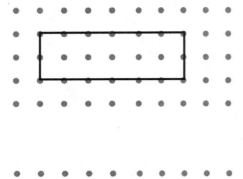

....

17 Draw a line of symmetry on each of these pictures.

18 Draw the other side of the picture.
Talk about what you did.

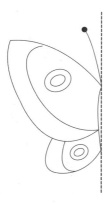

....

19 Use connecting cubes of 2 colors. Make a pattern.
Tell how your pattern repeats.

....

20 Tell how this pattern repeats. _____

Use these same objects to draw a new pattern.
Repeat 2 times.

STOP

Choose the correct answer.

 1

$6 + 4 =$ _____

(A) 9   (C) 12

(B) 11   (D) NOT HERE

2

$$\begin{array}{r} 4 \\ +4 \\ \hline \end{array}$$

(F) 6   (H) 8

(G) 7   (J) NOT HERE

 3

$$\begin{array}{r} 3 \\ 5 \\ +2 \\ \hline \end{array}$$

(A) 9   (C) 12

(B) 10   (D) NOT HERE

4

$$\begin{array}{r} 9 \\ 2 \\ +1 \\ \hline \end{array}$$

(F) 10   (H) 12

(G) 11   (J) NOT HERE

5 Ben spent 7¢.
Jan spent 5¢.
How much did they
spend in all?

(A) 10¢   (C) 12¢

(B) 11¢   (D) 13¢

6 5 birds are eating.
6 more birds come to eat.
How many birds are
eating?

(F) 11 birds   (H) 13 birds

(G) 12 birds   (J) 14 birds

7 How many more fish than turtles are there?

$$\begin{array}{r} 10 \\ -\ 7 \\ \hline \end{array}$$

(A) 2   (C) 4
(B) 3   (D) 5

8 Which number sentence belongs in this fact family?

$11 - 4 = 7$
$11 - 7 = 4$
$7 + 4 = 11$

(F) $4 + 3 = 7$
(G) $4 + 7 = 11$
(H) $11 - 6 = 5$
(J) $7 - 4 = 3$

9
$$\begin{array}{r} 7 \\ +2 \\ \hline 9 \end{array} \qquad \begin{array}{r} 9 \\ -2 \\ \hline \end{array}$$

(A) 6   (C) 8
(B) 7   (D) NOT HERE

10

5 6 7 8 9 10 11 12

$11 - 5 = \underline{\hspace{1cm}}$

(F) 4   (H) 6
(G) 5   (J) NOT HERE

11 Which number sentence does the story show?

Carlos had 12 apples.
He gave away 5.
How many are left?

(A) $12 - 5 = 7$
(B) $2 + 3 = 5$
(C) $12 - 7 = 5$
(D) NOT HERE

12 Which number sentence does the story show?

Ana had 4 fish.
She got 8 more.
How many does she have?

(F) $12 - 4 = 8$
(G) $4 + 4 = 8$
(H) $12 - 8 = 4$
(J) $4 + 8 = 12$

13 Show how to make a sum of 12 in 4 different ways.

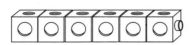 

____+____= ____   ____+____= ____

____+____= ____   ____+____= ____

....

14 Use cubes to find 3 numbers that add to 11.
Draw a picture.

Write the number sentence.

____+____+____= 11

....

15 Tell an addition story.
Write the number sentence.
Solve.

7 books

5 books

____+____= ____

16 Read the story. Draw a picture to solve it.

Nine students each need a pencil.

There are 5 pencils.

How many more pencils are needed?

_____ pencils

17 Use these cubes.

Write the sum.

$$8 \quad + \quad 3 \quad = \_\_\_$$

Write three more facts from this family.

___+___= ___   ___+___= ___

___+___= ___

18 Write the missing number.
Use cubes in the ten frame to help.

$$12 - \boxed{} = 7$$

GO ON

19 Write the number sentence for the story.

A pet store has 11 dogs and 6 cats.

How many more dogs than cats are there?

____ ⃝ ____ = ____

....

20 Solve. Write the number sentence.

Ann grew 11 carrots.

Brandon grew 7 carrots.

How many more carrots did Ann grow?

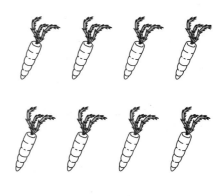

____ ⃝ ____ = ____

STOP

Choose the correct answer.

1 How many?

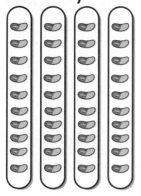

- Ⓐ 3 ones = 3
- Ⓑ 3 tens = 30
- Ⓒ 4 tens = 40
- Ⓓ 5 tens = 50

2 How many?

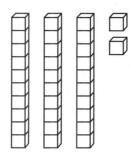

- Ⓕ 1 ten + 3 ones = 13
- Ⓖ 3 tens + 2 ones = 32
- Ⓗ 3 tens + 3 ones = 33
- Ⓙ NOT HERE

3 How many?

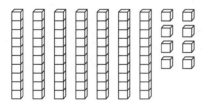

- Ⓐ 78
- Ⓒ 87
- Ⓑ 80
- Ⓓ NOT HERE

4 Jan picked a number **between** 55 and 57. Which number did she pick?

- Ⓕ 54
- Ⓗ 58
- Ⓖ 56
- Ⓙ 60

5 Which number comes just **before** 97?

_____, 97

- Ⓐ 79
- Ⓒ 90
- Ⓑ 87
- Ⓓ 96

6 Which is the better estimate?

- Ⓕ more than ten
- Ⓖ fewer than ten

GO ON

7 Which number is **greater**?

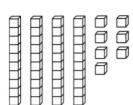

Ⓐ 47   Ⓑ 34

8 Which numbers are in order from **least** to **greatest**?

Ⓕ 64, 53, 42, 31
Ⓖ 15, 39, 27, 84
Ⓗ 32, 46, 57, 66

9 Count by twos. Which number comes **after** 14?

Ⓐ 12   Ⓒ 15
Ⓑ 13   Ⓓ 16

10 Count by tens. Which number comes **after** 50?

Ⓕ 40   Ⓗ 60
Ⓖ 51   Ⓙ NOT HERE

11 Count by fives. Which number comes **after** 35?

Ⓐ 30   Ⓒ 40
Ⓑ 36   Ⓓ 45

12 Even or odd?

11

Ⓕ even   Ⓖ odd

© Harcourt

13 These two pictures show 30.

What is another way to show 30?

Draw it here.

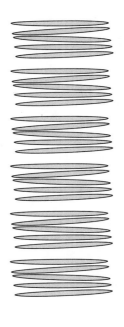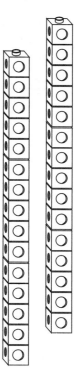

14 How many crackers on each tray?

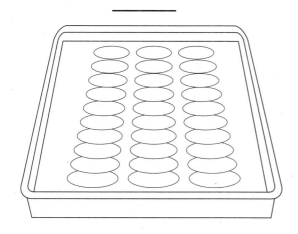 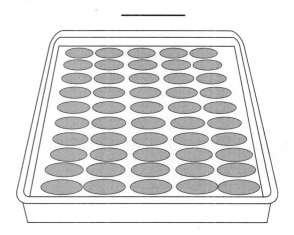

Circle the tray that has more.

Draw a line under the tray that has fewer.

Name _____

15 Write the numbers.
Circle the number
that is the greatest.

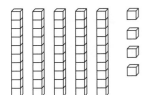

_____

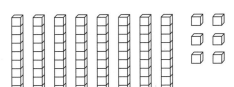

_____

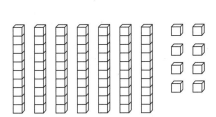

_____

16 Use cubes or base-ten blocks to show each number.

54   24   74   48

Write the numbers in order from least to greatest.

_____   _____   _____   _____

17 Estimate the number of fish.
about _____ fish
How did you estimate?

_____

_____

_____

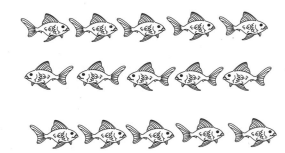

© Harcourt

Math Advantage Georgia Test Prep   28

GO ON ➡

18 Write the missing numbers.

1	2	3	4		6	7	8	9	
11	12	13	14		16	17	18	19	
21	22	23	24		26	27	28	29	
31	32	33	34		36	37	38	39	

Talk about the patterns you see.

19 Color squares to show 12.

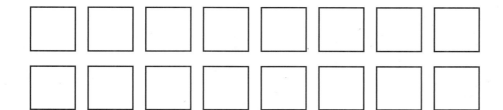

Circle even or odd.   even   odd

Tell how you know.

20 Draw a model to show that 7 is an odd number.

Tell about it.

STOP

Name _____

Choose the correct answer.

1 What is the value of this coin?

Ⓐ 1¢   Ⓒ 5¢
Ⓑ 2¢   Ⓓ 10¢

2 What is the name of this coin?

Ⓕ penny   Ⓗ quarter
Ⓖ nickel   Ⓙ dime

3 Which amount do these coins add up to?

Ⓐ 8¢   Ⓒ 14¢
Ⓑ 10¢   Ⓓ NOT HERE

4 Which amount do these coins add up to?

Ⓕ 4¢   Ⓗ 21¢
Ⓖ 16¢   Ⓙ 26¢

5 Which coins have the same value as ?

Ⓐ 1 dime, 1 nickel
Ⓑ 2 dimes, 1 nickel
Ⓒ 2 dimes, 2 pennies
Ⓓ 3 dimes, 5 pennies

6 Which toy can you buy with

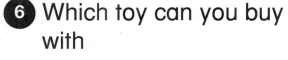 ?

Ⓕ 37¢   Ⓗ 32¢

Ⓖ 28¢   Ⓙ 41¢

Name _____

Use the calendar to answer questions 7, 8, and 9.

December

S	M	T	W	T	F	S
				1	2	3
4	5	6	7	8	9	10
11	12	13	14	15	16	17
18	19	20	21	22	23	24
25	26	27	28	29	30	31

---

7 On which day is December 17?

(A) Friday   (C) Sunday

(B) Saturday   (D) Monday

---

8 How many days are there in 1 week?

(F) 3 days   (H) 6 days

(G) 5 days   (J) 7 days

---

9 What is the date of the last Tuesday?

(A) December 20

(B) December 27

(C) December 28

(D) December 30

---

10 About how long does it take to do this?

(F) a minute   (H) a week

(G) an hour   (J) a month

---

11 Which clock shows the same time?

(A) 1:00   (C) 3:00

(B) 2:00   (D) NOT HERE

---

12 What time is it?

(F) 9:30   (H) 10:30

(G) 10:00   (J) NOT HERE

GO ON

13 Use pennies or cubes to model.

5¢

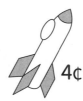

4¢

Draw how many pennies.

Write the total amount.

_____ ¢ + _____ ¢ = _____ ¢

14 You have 6¢.

What can you buy?

Draw your answer.

Write the number
sentence.

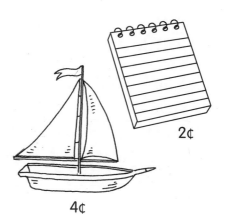

2¢

4¢

_____ ¢ ◯ _____ ¢ = _____ ¢

© Harcourt

GO ON ➡

15 Count the money.
Write the amount.

_____ ¢

16 Model with pennies.

You have 10¢.

You use 2¢ to buy a pencil.

Write a number sentence.   _____¢ – _____¢ = _____¢

GO ON

Name _____

17 Write the missing numbers on the calendar.

Tell how you know what to write.

March

Sunday	Monday	Tuesday	Wednesday	Thursday	Friday	Saturday
1	2	3	4		6	7
	9	10	11	12		14
15	16	17		19	20	
22	23	24	25		27	28
29		31				

....

18 Tell how these clocks are alike and different.

Show 6 o'clock on these clocks.

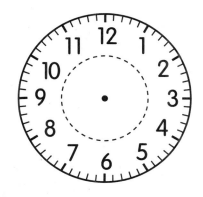   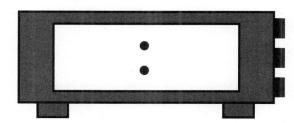

19 Draw two things you like to do.
Circle which takes longer.

· ·

20 The baby took a nap at 2 o'clock.
He woke up at 4 o'clock.
For how many hours did he sleep?

_____ hours

STOP

Name _____

Choose the correct answer.

1 About how many  long?

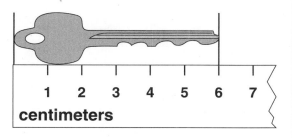

Ⓐ about 1   Ⓒ about 3

Ⓑ about 2   Ⓓ about 4

2 How many inches long?

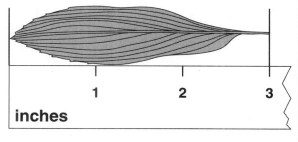

Ⓕ 1 inch   Ⓗ 3 inches

Ⓖ 2 inches   Ⓙ 4 inches

3 How many centimeters long?

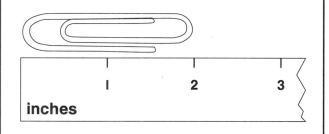

Ⓐ 3 centimeters

Ⓑ 4 centimeters

Ⓒ 5 centimeters

Ⓓ 6 centimeters

4 How many inches long?

Ⓕ 1 inch

Ⓖ 2 inches

Ⓗ 3 inches

Ⓙ 4 inches

Use the pictures to answer questions 5 and 6.

5 Which is the lightest?

Ⓐ   Ⓑ   Ⓒ

6 Which is the heaviest?

Ⓕ   Ⓖ   Ⓗ

GO ON ➡

7 What would you use to measure the length of this?

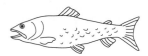

 A    **B**
inches

8 What would you use to measure the weight of this?

 F    **G**
centimeters

9 Which figure shows one-half?

 A   **C**

 B   **D**

10 Which figure shows one-fourth?

 F   **H**

 G   **J**

11 Which picture shows $\frac{1}{4}$ of the strawberries colored?

 A

 B

 C

 D

12 Which picture shows 1 of the candles lit?

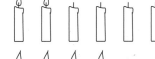 **F**

 **G**

 **H**

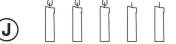 **J**

GO ON

13 How long is a bus?

What is the best object to use to find out?

Tell why.

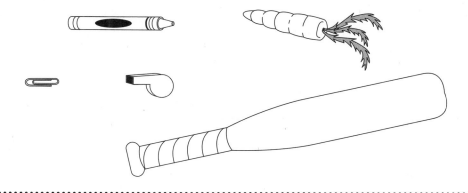

14 Find two objects to compare. Draw them.

Which is longer? How do you know?

15 Draw pictures. Compare.

Tell how you know.

These are longer than my arm.	These are shorter than my arm.

GO ON ➡

16 Draw 2 things you can measure with a ruler.
Tell how you can measure each one.

· ·

17 Use paper clips to measure the crayon. ____ paper clips
Then use a centimeter ruler. ____ centimeters
Are the measurements the same or different?
Why?

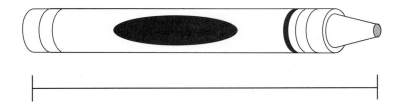

· ·

18 Which is heavier, the box or the airplane? _____
How do you know?

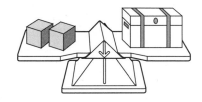 

GO ON

19 Which container holds more?

Which container holds less?

How do you know?

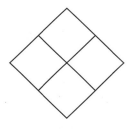

20 Draw a circle around each shape that shows fourths.

Tell why the shapes you circled show fourths.

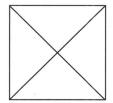
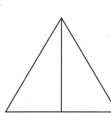

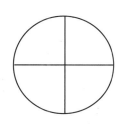

STOP

Choose the correct answer.

1 How are the dogs sorted?

Ⓐ big–little
Ⓑ black–white
Ⓒ round–square
Ⓓ NOT HERE

2 How many dogs are white?

	Tally Marks	Total
black	II	2
white	IIII	4

Ⓕ 1   Ⓗ 2
Ⓖ 3   Ⓙ NOT HERE

Use the tally table and the graph to answer questions 3 to 6.

	Favorite Toys	Total
truck	III	3
doll	I	I
drum	IIII	
ball	II	2

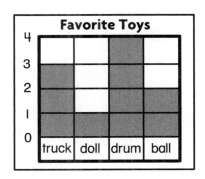

Favorite Toys

3 Which number is missing from the tally table?

Ⓐ 2   Ⓒ 4
Ⓑ 3   Ⓓ NOT HERE

4 How many children like dolls the best?

Ⓕ 1 child   Ⓗ 6 children
Ⓖ 4 children   Ⓙ NOT HERE

5 Which toy do children like the best?

Ⓐ truck   Ⓒ drum
Ⓑ doll   Ⓓ ball

6 How many more children like drums than dolls?

Ⓕ 1 child   Ⓗ 3 children
Ⓖ 2 children   Ⓙ NOT HERE

Name _____

Use the graph for questions 7 and 8.

Balls					Total
baseball	⚾	⚾	⚾		3
football	🏈				1
soccer ball	⚽	⚽	⚽	⚽	4

7 How many footballs are there?
- Ⓐ 1 football
- Ⓑ 2 footballs
- Ⓒ 3 footballs
- Ⓓ 4 footballs

8 How many balls in all?
- Ⓕ 5 balls
- Ⓖ 6 balls
- Ⓗ 7 balls
- Ⓙ 8 balls

Use the graph for questions 9 to 12.

Our Pets		Total
dog	🐕 🐕 🐕 🐕 🐕 🐕	6
cat	🐈 🐈 🐈 🐈	4
fish	🐟 🐟 🐟	3

9 How many children have fish?

- Ⓐ 2 children
- Ⓒ 4 children
- Ⓑ 3 children
- Ⓓ 5 children

10 How many more children have dogs than cats?

- Ⓕ 1 child
- Ⓗ 3 children
- Ⓖ 2 children
- Ⓙ 4 children

11 How many more children have dogs than fish?

- Ⓐ 1 child
- Ⓒ 3 children
- Ⓑ 2 children
- Ⓓ NOT HERE

12 How many pets do the children have in all?

- Ⓕ 10 pets
- Ⓗ 12 pets
- Ⓖ 11 pets
- Ⓙ 13 pets

Math Advantage Georgia Test Prep   44   **GO ON**

© Harcourt

13 Sort the shapes.

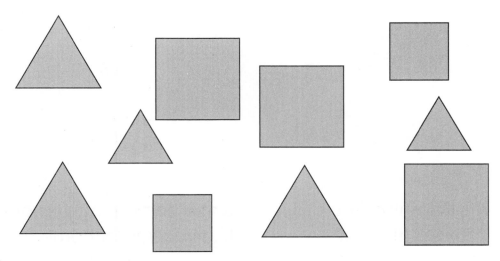

Make a table.

Shapes	Tally Marks	Total

14 Use the graph to answer the question.

Which sport do most children like best?

_____

Our Favorite Sports				
soccer	⚽	⚽		
basketball	🏀	🏀	🏀	
baseball	⚾	⚾	⚾	⚾

15 Circle which you are more likely to see.

Draw something you are likely to see at home.

Draw something you are not likely to see at home.

....

16 Georgine spun this pointer.

This chart shows the outcome of 10 spins.

Pointer Spins	
dark	II II
light	⊦⊦⊦ I

What do you think will happen if Georgine spins the pointer 20 times? _____

_____

17 This pointer can stop on 1, 2, or 3.

Which number is the pointer most likely to stop on?

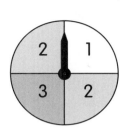

_____

18 Get some coins.

Sort them.

Make a graph.

Talk about the graph.

Coins								
pennies								
nickels								
dimes								

19 What does the graph show?

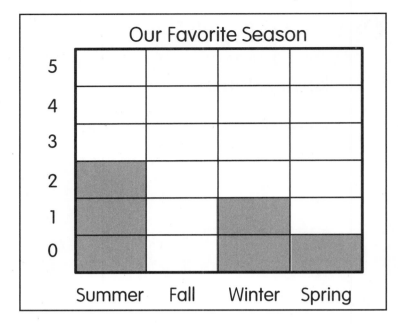

Our Favorite Season

| | Summer | Fall | Winter | Spring |

20 Ms. Garcia's class did a survey of their favorite juices. Here are the results.

Our Favorite Juices	
orange	||||
grape	⊞ |
apple	⊞ ⊞

Use the tallies to make a bar graph.

Our Favorite Juices

orange										
grape										
apple										
	1	2	3	4	5	6	7	8	9	10

STOP

© Harcourt

Name _____

Choose the correct answer.

1

$4 + 4 = 8$

$4 + 3 =$ _____

(A) 5 (C) 7
(B) 6 (D) 8

2

$\begin{array}{r} 9 \\ + 9 \\ \hline 18 \end{array}$ $\begin{array}{r} 9 \\ + 8 \\ \hline \end{array}$

(F) 16 (H) 18
(G) 17 (J) 19

3

$7 + 8 =$ _____

(A) 12 (C) 14
(B) 13 (D) NOT HERE

4

$6 + 7 =$ _____

(F) 13 (H) 15
(G) 14 (J) NOT HERE

5 Jenna had some hats.
Joe gave her 3 more.
Now she has 6.

How many hats did she
have to start?

(A) 2 caps (C) 4 caps
(B) 3 caps (D) 5 caps

6

$5 + 5 =$ _____

$10 - 5 = 5$

(F) 8   (H) 10
(G) 9   (J) 12

© Harcourt

7 Make a 10. Then add.

$$\begin{array}{r} 8 \\ + 6 \\ \hline \end{array}$$

Ⓐ 11   Ⓒ 13
Ⓑ 12   Ⓓ 14

8

$$\begin{array}{r} 9 \\ + 6 \\ \hline \end{array}$$

Ⓕ 14   Ⓗ 16
Ⓖ 15   Ⓙ NOT HERE

9

$$\begin{array}{r} 4 \\ 4 \\ + 7 \\ \hline \end{array}$$

Ⓐ 13   Ⓒ 15
Ⓑ 14   Ⓓ 16

10

$$\begin{array}{r} 7 \\ 3 \\ + 2 \\ \hline \end{array}$$

Ⓕ 12   Ⓗ 14
Ⓖ 13   Ⓙ 15

11

$$\begin{array}{r} 8 \\ + 7 \\ \hline 15 \end{array}$$ $$\begin{array}{r} 15 \\ - 7 \\ \hline \end{array}$$

Ⓐ 5   Ⓒ 7
Ⓑ 6   Ⓓ 8

12

$$\begin{array}{r} 9 \\ + 4 \\ \hline 13 \end{array}$$ $$\begin{array}{r} 13 \\ - 4 \\ \hline \end{array}$$

Ⓕ 6   Ⓗ 8
Ⓖ 7   Ⓙ 9

© Harcourt

13 Read the story. Then write a number sentence to solve.

There are 7 red apples and 6 yellow apples in the bowl.
How many apples are there in all?

_____ + _____ = _____

....

14 Draw ◯ to show 5 + 5.

Write the sum. 5 + 5 = _____

Draw ◯ to show 5 + 4.

Write the addition sentence. _____ + _____ = _____

GO ON

15 Write a number sentence.

Solve the problem.

Sam has 14 airplanes.

Sue has 7 airplanes.

How many more airplanes does Sam have than Sue?

_____ − _____ = _____

16 Draw counters in the ten-frames.

Show how you find the sum.

$$\begin{array}{r} 7 \\ + 9 \\ \hline \end{array}$$

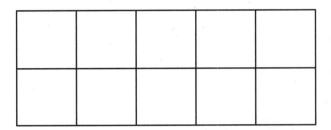

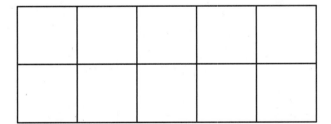

17 Solve the problem.

Six children are in the lunch line.

Two children get out of the line.

Then two new children get in the line.

How many children are in the lunch line now? _____ children

GO ON

© Harcourt

18 Write a number sentence. Solve.

Pablo gave Kristen 4 crayons.

Now Kristen has 12 crayons.

How many crayons did she have to start?

_____ + _____ = _____

19 What is the missing addend?

$5 + \boxed{} = 11$

Draw cubes to show.

20 What is the missing addend?

$9 + \boxed{} = 16$

Draw a picture to show.

STOP

Choose the correct answer.

1 How many counters?

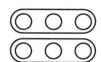

Ⓐ 3 counters   Ⓒ 6 counters
Ⓑ 5 counters   Ⓓ 8 counters

2 How many in each group?

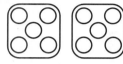

Ⓕ 4 counters   Ⓗ 6 counters
Ⓖ 5 counters   Ⓙ 7 counters

3 How many in each group?

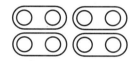

Ⓐ 2 counters   Ⓒ 6 counters
Ⓑ 4 counters   Ⓓ 8 counters

4 How many groups?

Ⓕ 2 groups   Ⓗ 4 groups
Ⓖ 3 groups   Ⓙ 5 groups

5 There are 3 groups.
Each group has 3
counters.

How many counters are
there in all?

Ⓐ 3 counters   Ⓒ 8 counters
Ⓑ 6 counters   Ⓓ 9 counters

6 There are 2 cars.
Each has 4 people in it.

How many people are
there in all?

Ⓕ 2 people
Ⓖ 4 people
Ⓗ 6 people
Ⓙ 8 people

GO ON ➡

7 Add.

tens	ones

$$\begin{array}{r} 20 \\ + 10 \\ \hline \end{array}$$

Ⓐ 3   Ⓒ 30
Ⓑ 20   Ⓓ 31

8 Add.

tens	ones

$$\begin{array}{r} 5\ \ 5 \\ + 2\ \ 1 \\ \hline \end{array}$$

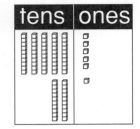

Ⓕ 6   Ⓗ 86
Ⓖ 76   Ⓙ NOT HERE

9 Add.

tens	ones

$$\begin{array}{r} 3\ \ 3 \\ + 3\ \ 5 \\ \hline \end{array}$$

Ⓐ 14   Ⓒ 68
Ⓑ 67   Ⓓ 86

10 Subtract.

tens	ones

$$\begin{array}{r} 4\ \ 5 \\ - 3\ \ 4 \\ \hline \end{array}$$

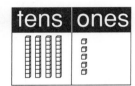

Ⓕ 11   Ⓗ 19
Ⓖ 12   Ⓙ 79

11 Subtract.

tens	ones

$$\begin{array}{r} 6\ \ 4 \\ - 2\ \ 1 \\ \hline \end{array}$$

Ⓐ 3   Ⓒ 35
Ⓑ 33   Ⓓ 43

12 Choose the answer that makes sense.

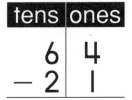

Joe had 49 pennies. He gave 25 pennies to Jill. How many pennies does he have left?

Ⓕ 4   Ⓗ 64
Ⓖ 24   Ⓙ 240

GO ON

© Harcourt

13 Draw. Use ◯. Make 2 groups.

Put 5 ◯ in each group.

How many ◯ are there in all? _____

....

14 Draw. Use 10 ◯.

Make 5 equal groups.

How many ◯ are in each group? _____

GO ON

15 Draw 12 ◯. Put 6 in each group.

How many groups did you make?   _____ groups

....

16 Draw a picture to solve.

There are 15 stars. They are in 5 equal groups.

How many stars are in each group?

_____ stars

....

17 Nat saved 38 pennies last month.

He saved 54 pennies this month.

How many pennies did Nat save in all?

_____ pennies

GO ON ➤

18 Use base-ten blocks and solve.

There are 27 ducks in the pond.

18 swim away.

How many ducks are left?

_____ ducks

19 How much money would you need to buy both?

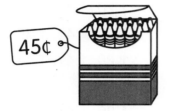

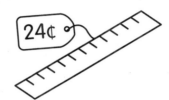

Choose the operation and solve. Write + or –.

$\bigcirc$ 45 ¢

24 ¢

_____

20 Add or subtract to solve the problem.

You have 75¢.

You buy a fish.

How much money do you have left?

_____ ¢

STOP

Georgia Quality Core Curriculum Objectives

1.20 Selects the numeral that names a group of objects and matches a group of objects with the appropriate numeral for a given set containing 0 through 100 objects.

1.41 Uses appropriate mathematical symbols (+, –, =).

1.44 Relates addition and subtraction to words, pictures, and concrete models, particularly sums and differences to 18 and related differences, and multiples of ten.

1.45 Determines addition and subtraction facts up to 18 using strategies such as counting all of a set, part-whole, counting on, counting back, counting up, doubles, property of zero, and commutativity of addition.

Item Numbers	Georgia QCC Objectives
1. A	1.20, 1.44, 1.45
2. H	1.20, 1.44, 1.45
3. C	1.20, 1.44, 1.45
4. J	1.20, 1.44, 1.45
5. D	1.20, 1.44, 1.45
6. G	1.20, 1.44, 1.45
7. C	1.20, 1.44, 1.45
8. G	1.20, 1.44, 1.45
9. B	1.20, 1.44, 1.45
10. F	1.20, 1.44, 1.45
11. C	1.20, 1.41, 1.44, 1.45
12. F	1.20, 1.41, 1.44, 1.45

13.   Answer: 4

3 + 1 = 4

Discussion

Tip: How will the number of counters change by adding one more counter?

Have children count out loud the number of counters on the page. Then have children

- draw one more counter.
- count on one more.

"Start at 3. Count on 1. **3, 4.**"

Then give the children 4 counters each and ask them to model how they solved the problem.

1.20 Selects the numeral that names a group of objects and matches a group of objects with the appropriate numeral for a given set containing 0 through 100 objects.

1.44 Relates addition and subtraction to words, pictures, and concrete models, particularly sums and differences to 18 and related differences, and multiples of ten.

14.   Answer: 6

4 + 2 = 6

Discussion

Tip: How could you use the picture to find out how many counters there are in all?

Some children may suggest counting all of the circles. Others may suggest starting with the group of four and counting on the two black circles.

1.20 Selects the numeral that names a group of objects and matches a group of objects with the appropriate numeral for a given set containing 0 through 100 objects.

1.44 Relates addition and subtraction to words, pictures, and concrete models, particularly sums and differences to 18 and related differences, and multiples of ten.

1.45 Determines addition and subtraction facts up to 18 using strategies such as counting all of a set, part-whole, counting on, counting back, counting up, doubles, property of zero, and commutativity of addition.

15.   Answer: 4 dots

2 + 2 = 4

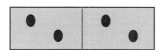

Discussion

Tip: How can you learn how many dots there are in all?

Talk about strategies like counting on from 2. Then have children

- draw 2 dots on one half domino and 2 on the other half.
- put a counter on each dot.
- count the counters.

Then hand out dominoes and ask children to tell how the 2 parts of a domino can show addition.

1.20 Selects the numeral that names a group of objects and matches a group of objects with the appropriate numeral for a given set containing 0 through 100 objects.

1.44 Relates addition and subtraction to words, pictures, and concrete models, particularly sums and differences to 18 and related differences, and multiples of ten.

1.45 Determines addition and subtraction facts up to 18 using strategies such as counting all of a set, part-whole, counting on, counting back, counting up, doubles, property of zero, and commutativity of addition.

16. Answer: 3
$$4 - 1 = 3$$

Discussion

Tip: How many triangles do you need to cross out to find out how many will be left?

Have children place a counter on each of the triangles. Then have children

- take away one counter.
- cross out the triangle that was beneath the counter.

Then ask children to explain how they could use addition to check their answers.

1.20 Selects the numeral that names a group of objects and matches a group of objects with the appropriate numeral for a given set containing 0 through 100 objects.

1.44 Relates addition and subtraction to words, pictures, and concrete models, particularly sums and differences to 18 and related differences, and multiples of ten.

1.45 Determines addition and subtraction facts up to 18 using strategies such as counting all of a set, part-whole, counting on, counting back, counting up, doubles, property of zero, and commutativity of addition.

17. Answer: 4
$$6 - 2 = 4$$

Discussion

Tip: Are you joining groups or taking away?

Ask children to tell how they decided whether to add or subtract to solve the problem. Discuss subtraction clues, such as "cross out," "difference," and the minus sign.

1.20 Selects the numeral that names a group of objects and matches a group of objects with the appropriate numeral for a given set containing 0 through 100 objects.

1.44 Relates addition and subtraction to words, pictures, and concrete models, particularly sums and differences to 18 and related differences, and multiples of ten.

1.45 Determines addition and subtraction facts up to 18 using strategies such as counting all of a set, part-whole, counting on, counting back, counting up, doubles, property of zero, and commutativity of addition.

18. Answer: 5 – 3 = 2

Discussion

Tip: How do you know which number to start the subtraction sentence with?

Have children use connecting cubes to model the subtraction story. Then have children

- tell you how many cubes they have to start with.
- take away 3 cubes and count how many cubes are left.

Ask children to explain how they used the cubes to help them write the subtraction sentence.

1.20 Selects the numeral that names a group of objects and matches a group of objects with the appropriate numeral for a given set containing 0 through 100 objects.

1.44 Relates addition and subtraction to words, pictures, and concrete models, particularly sums and differences to 18 and related differences, and multiples of ten.

1.45 Determines addition and subtraction facts up to 18 using strategies such as counting all of a set, part-whole, counting on, counting back, counting up, doubles, property of zero, and commutativity of addition.

19. Answer: 4
   $5 - 1 = 4$

Discussion

Tip: How can you use a calculator to help you subtract?

Have children press the 5 key on the calculator. Then have children

- press the minus key.
- press the number 1 key.
- press the = key.

Then ask, "How could you use the calculator to check your answer?"

1.20 Selects the numeral that names a group of objects and matches a group of objects with the appropriate numeral for a given set containing 0 through 100 objects.

1.44 Relates addition and subtraction to words, pictures, and concrete models, particularly sums and differences to 18 and related differences, and multiples of ten.

1.45 Determines addition and subtraction facts up to 18 using strategies such as counting all of a set, part-whole, counting on, counting back, counting up, doubles, property of zero, and commutativity of addition.

20. Answer: 5 trucks

Discussion

Tip: Are you joining groups or taking away?

Have children

- use 6 counters to show the number of trucks.
- take 1 counter away.
- count how many are left.
- draw 6 counters and cross 1 out.

Then ask children how they knew whether to add or subtract.

1.20 Selects the numeral that names a group of objects and matches a group of objects with the appropriate numeral for a given set containing 0 through 100 objects.

1.41 Uses appropriate mathematical symbols (+, –, =).

1.44 Relates addition and subtraction to words, pictures, and concrete models, particularly sums and differences to 18 and related differences, and multiples of ten.

1.45 Determines addition and subtraction facts up to 18 using strategies such as counting all of a set, part-whole, counting on, counting back, counting up, doubles, property of zero, and commutativity of addition.

Georgia Quality Core Curriculum Objectives

1.25 Recognizes different names for whole numbers through 20 (e.g., 4 = 2 + 2, 4 = 3 + 1, 4 = 0 + 4).

1.30 Recognizes equivalent and nonequivalent sets using one-to-one correspondence.

1.38 Recalls addition facts (sums to 18) and related subtraction facts presented vertically and horizontally (rewrite vertically),

1.42 Uses concrete objects to explore the commutative property of addition.

1.43 Explores the property of zero in addition and subtraction.

1.44 Relates addition and subtraction to words, pictures, and concrete models, particularly sums and differences to 18 and related differences, and multiples of ten.

1.45 Determines addition and subtraction facts up to 18 using strategies such as counting all of a set, part-whole, counting on, counting back, counting up, doubles, property of zero, and commutativity of addition.

Item Numbers	Georgia QCC Objectives
1. D	1.44, 1.45
2. F	1.25, 1.42, 1.44
3. B	1.25, 1.44
4. H	1.44, 1.45
5. C	1.44, 1.45
6. G	1.30, 1.44, 1.45
7. C	1.44, 1.45
8. G	1.38, 1.45
9. A	1.43
10. J	1.43
11. B	1.44, 1.45
12. H	1.44, 1.45

13. Answer: Answers will vary, but may include 7 + 0 = 7, 6 + 1 = 7, 5 + 2 = 7, 4 + 3 = 7, 3 + 4 = 7, 2 + 5 = 7, 1 + 6 = 7, 0 + 7 = 7

Discussion

Tip: How many different names for 7 can you think of?

Have children say the different names for 7. Then have children

- choose one of the names for 7.
- use two different-colored crayons to color the counters.

Then ask children to write the number sentences for their illustrations.

1.24 Recognizes, writes, and orally names numerals 0 through 100.

1.25 Recognizes different names for whole numbers through 20 (e.g., 4 = 2 + 2, 4 = 3 + 1, 4 = 0 + 4).

1.44 Relates addition and subtraction to words, pictures, and concrete models, particularly sums and differences to 18 and related differences, and multiples of ten.

14. Answer: Possible answers: 0 + 10, 1 + 9, 2 + 8, 3 + 7, 4 + 6, 5 + 5, 6 + 4, 7 + 3, 8 + 2, 9 + 1, 10 + 0.

Discussion

Tip: How can you show the same number in different ways?

Have children

- toss 10 two-color counters.
- group the reds together and the yellows together.
- point to each group and say how many, such as "4 reds and 6 yellows."
- record the model as a number fact, such as 4 + 6 = 10.

Then ask children to show different names for 10 using the counters and a 10-frame.

1.24 Recognizes, writes, and orally names numerals 0 through 100.

1.25 Recognizes different names for whole numbers through 20 (e.g., 4 = 2 + 2, 4 = 3 + 1, 4 = 0 + 4).

1.41 Uses appropriate mathematical symbols (+, –, =)

1.44 Relates addition and subtraction to words, pictures, and concrete models, particularly sums and differences to 18 and related differences, and multiples of ten.

15. Answer: 5 + 5 = 10 (doubles); 4 + 3 = 7

Discussion

Tip: How many strawberries are there altogether? How many cones?

Have children

- add the sums.
- identify the doubles by looking for matching groups.

Ask what it means to add doubles.

1.44 Relates addition and subtraction to words, pictures, and concrete models, particularly sums and differences to 18 and related differences, and multiples of ten.

1.45 Determines addition and subtraction facts up to 18 using strategies such as counting all of a set, part-whole, counting on, counting back, counting up, doubles, property of zero, and commutativity of addition.

© Harcourt

16. Answer: 9

Discussion

Tip: Is this a story about joining flowers or comparing colors?

Have children

- draw a row of 6 flowers.
- draw a row of 3 flowers.
- tell how many flowers in all.

Ask how they could use a number line to solve the problem.

1.44 Relates addition and subtraction to words, pictures, and concrete models, particularly sums and differences to 18 and related differences, and multiples of ten.

1.45 Determines addition and subtraction facts up to 18 using strategies such as counting all of a set, part-whole, counting on, counting back, counting up, doubles, property of zero, and commutativity of addition.

17. Answer: 7

Discussion

Tip: How many are left?

Have children

- count all the squares.
- cover 10 squares with counters.
- take away 3 counters.
- count how many counters are left over.
- write a vertical sentence.

$$\begin{array}{r} 10 \\ -3 \\ \hline 7 \end{array}$$

Tell how you know $10 - 3 = 7$ in the vertical format is the same as $10 - 3 = 7$ in the horizontal format.

1.44 Relates addition and subtraction to words, pictures, and concrete models, particularly sums and differences to 18 and related differences, and multiples of ten.

1.45 Determines addition and subtraction facts up to 18 using strategies such as counting all of a set, part-whole, counting on, counting back, counting up, doubles, property of zero, and commutativity of addition.

18. Answer: See discussion below.

Discussion

Tip: What do you know about fact families? (They make addition and subtraction sentences.)

Have children

- count out 10 counters.
- make two groups with a different number of counters in each group.
- name the number of counters in each group and write an addition sentence.
- write a related subtraction sentence.

1.24 Recognizes, writes, and orally names numerals 0 through 100.

1.25 Recognizes different names for whole numbers through 20 (e.g., 4 = 2 + 2, 4 = 3 + 1, 4 = 0 + 4).

1.42 Uses concrete objects to explore the commutative property of addition.

© Harcourt

Math Advantage Georgia Test Prep   66   **Answer Keys**

19. Answer: 4
$7 - 3 = 4$

Discussion

Tip: Which direction on the number line do you move to subtract?

Give children a counter and ask them to place it on the number line on the 7. Then have children move the counter to the left as you count back 3.

Then ask children to explain why they moved the counter to the left on the number line rather than to the right.

1.39 Uses models such as base ten blocks, pictorial representation, and number line to explore adding and subtracting two-digit numbers without regrouping.

1.44 Relates addition and subtraction to words, pictures, and concrete models, particularly sums and differences to 18 and related differences, and multiples of ten.

1.45 Determines addition and subtraction facts up to 18 using strategies such as counting all of a set, part-whole, counting on, counting back, counting up, doubles, property of zero, and commutativity of addition.

20. Answer: 7 students $(1 + 6 = 7)$

Discussion

Tip: Is this a story about going away or about joining others?

Encourage children to draw 1 figure and then 6 figures on the picture. Then count on to solve.

Ask why they decided to use addition instead of subtraction. When groups are being joined, what do we know about their size?

1.20 Selects the numeral that names a group of objects and matches a group of objects with the appropriate numeral for a given set containing 0 through 100 objects.

1.44 Relates addition and subtraction to words, pictures, and concrete models, particularly sums and differences to 18 and related differences, and multiples of ten.

1.45 Determines addition and subtraction facts up to 18 using strategies such as counting all of a set, part-whole, counting on, counting back, counting up, doubles, property of zero, and commutativity of addition.

Georgia Quality Core Curriculum Objectives

1.3 Identifies circles, squares, triangles, ovals, diamonds, and rectangles in various orientations/positions.

1.4 Identifies spheres, cubes, and cones.

1.5 Identifies a specified positional relationship between objects, (before, after, between, near

1.6 Determines figures that are symmetrical by folding.

1.8 Compares or orders shapes by size (same size as, larger than, smaller than, largest, or smallest).

1.9 Identifies relationships (larger than, largest, smaller than, smallest, same size as, same shape as, inside, outside, on, left, and right).

1.31 Continues simple patterns such as those involving numbers, shapes, colors, seasons, and events.

Item Numbers	Georgia QCC Objectives
1. C	1.3
2. H	
3. B	1.4
4. J	1.3, 1.9
5. B	1.8, 1.9
6. F	1.3, 1.8, 1.9
7. A	1.5
8. H	1.5
9. B	1.6
10. F	1.5, 1.9
11. A	1.31
12. H	1.31

13. Answer: cube, rectangular prism, cylinder

Discussion

Tip: **What happens if you put a cone into the middle of a stack?**

Help children

- discover that a cone cannot support another block because it has only 1 flat face.

- recognize that if a shape does not have 2 flat faces, it will not stack.

14. Answer: can, hat

Discussion

Tip: **Describe the faces that you see on each object.**

Have children

- check each shape for flat faces.

- discuss the difference between a curved face and a round, flat face.

15. Answer: triangle or square for pyramid, rectangle for rectangular prism, square for cube

Discussion

Tip: **Compare the shapes to the faces of each solid figure.**

Have children recall plane shapes that correspond to solid figures. They should be familiar with these from real-life experiences and previous test questions.

1.3 Identifies circles, squares, triangles, ovals, diamonds, and rectangles in various orientations/positions.

16. Answer: any rectangle that is 7 dots by 3 dots

1.9 Identifies relationships (larger than, largest, smaller than, smallest, same size as, same shape as, inside, outside, on, left, and right).

Discussion

Tip: How is the dot paper helpful?

Have children

- identify the shape as a rectangle with 4 sides and 4 corners.

- count the dots on one side.

- draw the rectangle using the same number of dots.

- check the drawing.

- change if necessary.

Ask children how they can tell if their drawings are correct.

17. Answer: The line of symmetry for the scissors is diagonal since the scissors are viewed at an angle. The lines of symmetry for the face, shirt, and bucket are vertical.

1.6 Determines figures that are symmetrical by folding.

Discussion

Tip: Can any line be a line of symmetry?

Have children draw a line through each shape creating 2 sides that match. Ask what it means for a shape to have a line of symmetry.

Have children show why horizontal lines could not be lines of symmetry for these shapes.

18. Answer: drawing of complete butterfly

Discussion

Tip: Each half of a butterfly is the same size and shape.

To solve the problem, have children draw a mirror image of the butterfly on the other side of the line of symmetry.

Have children summarize what they know about symmetry.

1.6 Determines figures that are symmetrical by folding.

19. Answer: Will vary; sample solution: red, red, blue.

Discussion

Tip: Use cubes to decide on a pattern and then show it on paper.

Have students

- connect the cubes to create a pattern.
- after reproducing it, take turns "reading" patterns aloud.

Ask children what their patterns could be named. Typically the name includes the colors, shapes, letters, numbers, or objects that are repeated.

1.31 Continues simple patterns such as those involving numbers, shapes, colors, seasons, and events.

20. Answer: dime, penny, nickel (or 10-1-5); new patterns will vary.

Discussion

Tip: What other order can you show?

Have children

- identify the order shown.
- create a new pattern by varying the order of 1 or 2 objects.
- repeat the new pattern correctly by checking their work.

Encourage children to tell how their new patterns compare to the sample shown. For example, the sample is ordered by the increasing physical size of the coins. Perhaps another pattern reverses the order to decreasing size.

M.1.31 Continues simple patterns such as those involving numbers, shapes, colors, seasons, and events.

Georgia Quality Core Curriculum Objectives

M.1.30 Recognizes equivalent and nonequivalent sets using one-to-one correspondence.

M.1.37 Adds three 1-digit whole numbers presented vertically and horizontally (rewrite vertically) without regrouping.

M.1.38 Recalls addition facts (sums to 18) and related subtraction facts presented vertically and horizontally (rewrite vertically),

M.1.39 Uses models such as base ten blocks, pictorial representation, and number line to explore adding and subtracting two-digit numbers without regrouping.

M.1.40 Adds and subtracts 2-digit whole numbers without regrouping vertically and horizontally (rewrite vertically).

M.1.44 Relates addition and subtraction to words, pictures, and concrete models, particularly sums and differences to 18 and related differences, and multiples of ten.

M.1.45 Determines addition and subtraction facts up to 18 using strategies such as counting all of a set, part-whole, counting on, counting back, counting up, doubles, property of zero, and commutativity of addition.

Item Numbers	Georgia QCC Objectives
1. D	1.38
2. H	1.38, 1.45
3. B	1.37
4. H	1.37
5. C	1.38, 1.44, 1.45
6. F	1.44, 1.45
7. B	1.30, 1.44, 1.45
8. G	1.38, 1.40
9. B	1.38
10. H	1.39, 1.44, 1.45
11. A	1.38, 1.44
12. J	1.38, 1.44

13. Answer: Will vary

Discussion

Tip: How can you use objects to solve the problem?

Have children take 12 objects and put them into two groups. Then they can count the number in each group and write an addition sentence. Here are some possibilities:

Addition Patterns

11 + 1 = 12	1 + 11 = 12
10 + 2 = 12	2 + 10 = 12
9 + 3 = 12	3 + 9 = 12
8 + 4 = 12	4 + 8 = 12
7 + 5 = 12	5 + 7 = 12
6 + 6 = 12	same

Have children share their solutions. You may want to have them make an organized list and look for patterns.

M.1.24 Recognizes, writes, and orally names numerals 0 through 100.

M.1.25 Recognizes different names for whole numbers through 20 (e.g., 4 = 2 + 2, 4 = 3 + 1, 4 = 0 + 4).

M.1.42 Uses concrete objects to explore the commutative property of addition.

M.1.45 Determines addition and subtraction facts up to 18 using strategies such as counting all of a set, part-whole, counting on, counting back, counting up, doubles, property of zero, and commutativity of addition.

14. Answer: See discussion below.

Discussion

Tip: You can use counting on, doubles, or mental math as possible strategies.

Have children

- connect cubes to find a sum.

- either count on to 11 and record the number, or subtract to find the third number.

To use doubles, children would find the sum and count on or subtract. Children may or may not be aware of relative size, so if they start with a large number, they will need to have 2 small ones as the other addends. Ask children to explain how to find the sum of 3 numbers.

M.1.3 Identifies circles, squares, triangles, ovals, diamonds, and rectangles in various orientations/positions.

M.1.45 Determines addition and subtraction facts up to 18 using strategies such as counting all of a set, part-whole, counting on, counting back, counting up, doubles, property of zero, and commutativity of addition.

15. Answer: 7 + 5 = 12

Discussion

Tip: What are addition stories about?

Have students discuss what they know about addition stories. We use addition when we are joining groups. Ask what groups are in their stories and what happened to them.

Ask children to recommend a way someone could solve their story. Possible answers are to know addition combinations, make a drawing, write a number sentence, act it out, and make a model.

M.1.44 Relates addition and subtraction to words, pictures, and concrete models, particularly sums and differences to 18 and related differences, and multiples of ten.

M.1.45 Determines addition and subtraction facts up to 18 using strategies such as counting all of a set, part-whole, counting on, counting back, counting up, doubles, property of zero, and commutativity of addition.

16. Answer: 4 pencils

Discussion

Tip: How can you use connecting cubes to model the story?

You can show 9 students and 5 pencils. Then you can match 5 pencils with 5 children. Count the number of students without pencils. That's how many more pencils you need. Finally, children can draw a picture sentence such as:

$$9 \rightarrow - 5 \rightarrow = \boxed{} \rightarrow$$

$$5 \rightarrow + \boxed{} \rightarrow = 9 \rightarrow$$

M.1.44 Relates addition and subtraction to words, pictures, and concrete models, particularly sums and differences to 18 and related differences, and multiples of ten.

M.1.45 Determines addition and subtraction facts up to 18 using strategies such as counting all of a set, part-whole, counting on, counting back, counting up, doubles, property of zero, and commutativity of addition.

17. Answer: Will vary

Discussion

Tip: How can addition and subtraction fact families help you make up some number sentences?

Help children see that there are many possible fact families for 8 counters.

Have children use counters to model addition and subtraction sentences for each family they find, for example: $5 + 3 = 8$, $3 + 5 = 8$, $8 - 3 = 5$, $8 - 5 = 3$.

Encourage children to talk about their number sentences and describe the relationship between the addition and subtraction sentences in a fact family.

M.1.42 Uses concrete objects to explore the commutative property of addition.

18. Answer: 9

Discussion

Tip: How can you use connecting cubes to help you fill in the frame?

Have children use connecting cubes to model the subtraction problem. Children can place 12 connecting cubes in the frame Have them remove cubes one at a time until 7 cubes remain in the frame.

M.1.44 Relates addition and subtraction to words, pictures, and concrete models, particularly sums and differences to 18 and related differences, and multiples of ten.

M.1.45 Determines addition and subtraction facts up to 18 using strategies such as counting all of a set, part-whole, counting on, counting back, counting up, doubles, property of zero, and commutativity of addition.

19. Answer: There are 5 more dogs than cats.
11 – 6 = 5

Discussion

Tip: What are you asked to find?

Have children model the story using counters, make a drawing, or use fact families.

Discuss how to decide whether to add or subtract. When asked to compare groups to find a difference, we use subtraction.

M.1.41 Uses appropriate mathematical symbols (+, –, =).

M.1.44 Relates addition and subtraction to words, pictures, and concrete models, particularly sums and differences to 18 and related differences, and multiples of ten.

M.1.45 Determines addition and subtraction facts up to 18 using strategies such as counting all of a set, part-whole, counting on, counting back, counting up, doubles, property of zero, and commutativity of addition.

20. Answer: 11 – 7 = 4

Discussion

Tip: Use the picture to solve the problem.

Have children model the story using counters, make a drawing, or use fact families. Discuss how to decide whether to add or subtract. When asked to compare groups to find a difference, we use subtraction.

M.1.41 Uses appropriate mathematical symbols (+, –, =).

M.1.44 Relates addition and subtraction to words, pictures, and concrete models, particularly sums and differences to 18 and related differences, and multiples of ten.

M.1.45 Determines addition and subtraction facts up to 18 using strategies such as counting all of a set, part-whole, counting on, counting back, counting up, doubles, property of zero, and commutativity of addition.

© Harcourt

Georgia Quality Core Curriculum Objectives

1.1 Explores estimation of quantities of less than 100.

1.5 Identifies a specified positional relationship between objects, (before, after, between, near

1.20 Selects the numeral that names a group of objects and matches a group of objects with the appropriate numeral for a given set containing 0 through 100 objects.

1.21 Counts by ones, fives, and tens to 100 and by twos to 20. Counts backwards from 20.

1.22 Models and pictorially represents whole numbers through 100 using groups of tens and ones and orally names numbers (e.g., 3 tens, 2 ones; thirty-two; or 30 + 2 = 32).

1.27 Identifies place value by determining number of tens and ones in a given number.

1.28 Identifies numerical relations (greater than, less than, equal to) of numbers 0 through 100 and sequences of numbers in ascending order.

1.30 Recognizes equivalent and nonequivalent sets using one-to-one correspondence.

Item Numbers	Georgia QCC Objectives
1. C	1.20, 1.22, 1.27
2. G	1.20, 1.22, 1.27
3. A	1.20, 1.22, 1.27
4. G	1.5
5. D	
6. G	1.1
7. A	1.28
8. H	1.28
9. D	1.5, 1.21
10. H	1.5, 1.21
11. C	1.5, 1.21
12. G	1.30

13. Answer: Accept all correct answers.

Discussion

Tip: How can you arrange 30 counters so they are easy to count?

Have children

- take 30 counters.

- arrange the counters differently from the ways shown.

- draw a picture to show the arrangement.

- tell how the arrangement is different from the two shown.

- tell which arrangement is easiest to count and why.

Then ask children to describe another way they could have arranged the counters. Encourage discussion using number names and counting by 2s, 5s, and 10s.

14. Answer: 30 will be underlined and 50 will be circled.

Discussion

Tip: How can you count the crackers easily to find out which tray has more?

Have children

- point to a row of crackers and tell how many in the row.

- tell if each row has the same number of crackers.

- count aloud by tens to find out how many on each tray.

- compare the number of crackers on each tray.

Then ask children to show how they solved the problem.

Encourage discussion of how counting by tens made it easier than counting another way.

15. Answer: 54, 86, 78; 86 is the greatest

Discussion

Tip: How can you compare the numbers to see which is the greatest?

Have children

- point to each model, count tens and ones, and write the number.

- compare how many tens are in each number and tell which number is the greatest.

Then ask children to tell how they know which group is the greatest. Encourage a discussion of matching one-to-one and ordering strategies.

1.20 Selects the numeral that names a group of objects and matches a group of objects with the appropriate numeral for a given set containing 0 through 100 objects.

1.21 Counts by ones, fives, and tens to 100 and by twos to 20. Counts backwards from 20.

1.22 Models and pictorially represents whole numbers through 100 using groups of tens and ones and orally names numbers (e.g., 3 tens, 2 ones; thirty-two; or 30 + 2 = 32).

1.24 Recognizes, writes, and orally names numerals 0 through 100.

1.20 Selects the numeral that names a group of objects and matches a group of objects with the appropriate numeral for a given set containing 0 through 100 objects.

1.22 Models and pictorially represents whole numbers through 100 using groups of tens and ones and orally names numbers (e.g., 3 tens, 2 ones; thirty-two; or 30 + 2 = 32).

1.24 Recognizes, writes, and orally names numerals 0 through 100.

1.20 Selects the numeral that names a group of objects and matches a group of objects with the appropriate numeral for a given set containing 0 through 100 objects.

1.22 Models and pictorially represents whole numbers through 100 using groups of tens and ones and orally names numbers (e.g., 3 tens, 2 ones; thirty-two; or 30 + 2 = 32).

1.24 Recognizes, writes, and orally names numerals 0 through 100.

1.28 Identifies numerical relations (greater than, less than, equal to) of numbers 0 through 100 and sequences of numbers in ascending order.

© Harcourt

16. Answer: Children can model as follows:

   54 - Show 5 tens and 4 ones.

   24 - Show 2 tens and 4 ones.

   74 - Show 7 tens and 4 ones.

   48 - Show 4 tens and 8 ones.

   In order from least to greatest:

   24, 48, 54, 74

Discussion

Tip: How can you make models to show the size of whole numbers and compare them?

Have children

- point to each number and model how many tens and ones.

- identify which number has the fewest tens.

- identify which number has the most tens.

- order the models from fewest tens to most tens.

Then ask children to tell what "order from least to greatest" means.

Encourage discussion using "before," "after," and "between."

1.22 Models and pictorially represents whole numbers through 100 using groups of tens and ones and orally names numbers (e.g., 3 tens, 2 ones; thirty-two; or 30 + 2 = 32).

1.23 Translates word to numerals and numerals to words (0 through 20).

1.24 Recognizes, writes, and orally names numerals 0 through 100.1.1 Explores estimation of quantities of less than 100.

17. Answer: Possible answers: more than 10, more than 15, or fewer than 20.

Discussion

Tip: How can you estimate how many fish there are without counting?

Have children

- circle a subgroup in the picture to use as a benchmark.

- tell what the benchmark is. They might use 5 as a benchmark for this problem.

- tell how to use the benchmark to estimate how many fish there are.

Then ask children to tell how estimating is different from counting.

Encourage discussion of using a benchmark to estimate.

1.1 Explores estimation of quantities of less than 100.

18. Answer: The missing numbers are:
5, 10, 15, 20, 25, 30, 35, 40.
Children may say that every number they write ends in 5 or 0.

Discussion

Tip: How can counting by fives help you write in the missing numbers?

Have children

- point to the first numbers and softly count aloud, "1, 2, 3, 4."
- say the next number loudly, "5."
- continue by counting, "6, 7, 8, 9," softly and "10" loudly.
- follow the pattern and write each "loud" number in the chart.

Then ask children to describe a pattern and relationship they see among the numbers they wrote in each column. Encourage discussion that describes numerals in the tens place and the ones place. Have children tell about other patterns they see in the chart.

1.31 Continues simple patterns such as those involving numbers, shapes, colors, seasons, and events.

1.32 Sequences numbers and points on a number line and determines missing numerals (0 through 20).

---

19. Possible answer: Children may explain that 12 is an even number because everything is paired and there are none left over.

Discussion

Tip: How do you know if a number is odd or even?

Have children

- count 12 connecting cubes.
- snap them together in pairs.
- color the boxes to represent the snapped cubes.
- tell if there are any left over.

Then ask children to explain how they know 12 is an even number.

1.30 Recognizes equivalent and nonequivalent sets using one-to-one correspondence.

1.31 Continues simple patterns such as those involving numbers, shapes, colors, seasons, and events.

---

20. Answer: Accept all answers that show 6 paired items and 1 left over.

Discussion

Tip: How do you know if a number is odd or even?

Have children

- count 7 connecting cubes.
- arrange them in 3 pairs.
- draw squares to represent the cubes.
- tell if all the squares can be paired.

Then ask children to tell what math words they need to know to solve the problem.

Encourage discussion that includes the words "pairs" and "left over."

1.30 Recognizes equivalent and nonequivalent sets using one-to-one correspondence.

1.31 Continues simple patterns such as those involving numbers, shapes, colors, seasons, and events.

Answer Keys

Georgia Quality Core Curriculum Objectives

1.12 Names and identifies values of coins (penny, nickel, dime, quarter) and dollar bills.

1.13 Determines the value of a set of coins up to $0.50 using quarters, nickels, pennies, and dimes.

1.14 Determines equivalent values of coins up to $0.50.

1.15 Identifies days, weeks, and months on a calendar.

1.16 Identifies number of minutes in an hour, number of days in a week, and number of months in a year.

1.17 Selects appropriate units (minutes, hours, days, weeks, and months) and appropriate instruments (clocks and calendars) to measure time.

1.18 Tells time to the half-hour and hour.

Item Numbers	Georgia QCC Objectives
1. C	1.12
2. J	1.12
3. A	1.13
4. H	1.13
5. B	1.14
6. J	1.13
7. B	1.15
8. J	1.16
9. B	1.15
10. F	1.17
11. C	1.18
12. F	1.18

13. Answer: 9¢ (5¢ + 4¢)

Discussion

Tip: What will you do first?

Have children

- model the amounts for each item.
- join pennies or cubes.
- count the sum.

Ask children if they are separating or joining groups. Ask how they know their answers are right.

1.12 Names and identifies values of coins (penny, nickel, dime, quarter) and dollar bills.

1.13 Determines the value of a set of coins up to $0.50 using quarters, nickels, pennies, and dimes.

14. Answers may vary. Children may draw 1 notepad and 1 boat for 6¢ or 3 notepads for 6¢.

Discussion

Tip: Are you joining groups or taking away?

Have children model the story with 6 counters. Ask if anyone got a different answer since there are two possibilities.

Ask children to explain how they solved the problem. (Children can use addition or subtraction.)

1.12 Names and identifies values of coins (penny, nickel, dime, quarter) and dollar bills.

1.13 Determines the value of a set of coins up to $0.50 using quarters, nickels, pennies, and dimes.

1.41 Uses appropriate mathematical symbols (+, −, =).

1.45 Determines addition and subtraction facts up to 18 using strategies such as counting all of a set, part-whole, counting on, counting back, counting up, doubles, property of zero, and commutativity of addition.

15. Answer: 59¢ Observe as the child counts to see if he or she groups like coins together and counts by 1s, 2s, 5s, or 10s.

Discussion

Tip: How can you organize the coins to count them easily?

Have children

- identify pennies, nickels, and dimes.
- group like coins together.
- start with the dimes, count by tens, and then continue counting on by fives and ones as appropriate.

Then ask the child to explain how he or she solved the problem. Encourage discussion about the values of the coins using "more than" and "less than."

1.13 Determines the value of a set of coins up to $0.50 using quarters, nickels, pennies, and dimes.

© Harcourt

16. Answer:
$$10¢ - 2¢ = 8¢$$

Discussion

Tip: When you tell a subtraction story, do you want to know how many are left or how many in all?

Have children

- model spending money with their pennies.

- model 10 minus 2.

- count how many are left.

- tell a complete subtraction story.

- write a correct subtraction sentence.

Encourage discussion using the phrases "take away" and "minus" for "bought" or "spent."

1.12 Names and identifies values of coins (penny, nickel, dime, quarter) and dollar bills.

1.44 Relates addition and subtraction to words, pictures, and concrete models, particularly sums and differences to 18 and related differences, and multiples of ten.

1.45 Determines addition and subtraction facts up to 18 using strategies such as counting all of a set, part-whole, counting on, counting back, counting up, doubles, property of zero, and commutativity of addition.

17. Answer: See shaded boxes in calendar.

March

Sunday	Monday	Tuesday	Wednesday	Thursday	Friday	Saturday
1	2	3	4	5	6	7
8	9	10	11	12	13	14
15	16	17	18	19	20	21
22	23	24	25	26	27	28
29	30	31				

Discussion

Tip: How does knowing the order of numbers help you read a calendar?

Have children

- point to and read the numbers 1 to 4 aloud.

- tell what number comes after 4.

- write the number 5 on the calendar.

- continue to read the numbers aloud and fill in the missing numbers.

Have children describe another way they could have solved the problem. Encourage discussion using "before," "after," and "between" to reflect the order of numbers.

1.32 Sequences numbers and points on a number line and determines missing numerals (0 through 20).

© Harcourt

18. Answer: See discussion below.

Discussion

Tip: How do you tell time on a clock that has hands? How do you tell time on a clock that has no hands?

Have children

- point to the analog clock and tell which hand shows the hour.
- point to the digital clock and tell which number shows the hour.

Ask children to tell which clock is easier for them to read and why.

Children may say both clocks show the same time: 3:00. The analog clock shows all the numbers and has two hands that point to the numbers to show the time, while the digital clock only shows the numbers for the time.

 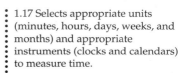

Children's clocks should correctly show six o'clock.

CHAPTERS 16–19
Test 6

1.18 Tells time to the half-hour and hour.

19. Answer: Accept all reasonable answers, such as drawings that show going to the movies (a longer time) and making popcorn (a shorter time).

Discussion

Tip: How can you act out the activities to see which one takes longer (or shorter)?

Have children

- draw pictures of two different things they like to do.
- close their eyes and imagine doing each thing.
- identify which takes more (or less) time.

Then ask children to tell why one activity takes a longer (or shorter) time than the other.

Encourage discussion that includes estimation of time.

1.17 Selects appropriate units (minutes, hours, days, weeks, and months) and appropriate instruments (clocks and calendars) to measure time.

20. Answer: 2 hours

Discussion

Tip: How can a clock help you solve the problem?

Children can show the time the baby started his nap on the clock, 2:00. Then they can move the hands on the clock to show when he got up, 4:00. The difference between the two times tells how long he slept.

1.18 Tells time to the half-hour and hour.

1.44 Relates addition and subtraction to words, pictures, and concrete models, particularly sums and differences to 18 and related differences, and multiples of ten.

© Harcourt

Georgia Quality Core Curriculum Objectives

1.2 Recognizes different ways of representing fractions using concrete and pictorial models and words for one-half and one-fourth.

1.9 Identifies relationships (larger than, largest, smaller than, smallest, same size as, same shape as, inside, outside, on, left, and right).

1.10 Describes, orders, and measures length using inches and centimeters.

1.11 Selects appropriate instrument for determining specified measurement of height, weight, capacity, and temperature.

1.19 Compares weight of two real objects (heavier than, lighter than) and capacity of two real containers (more than, less than) using both dry and liquid measure units, and compares the height of two real objects (shorter than, taller than).

Item Numbers	Georgia QCC Objectives
1. A	1.9
2. H	1.10
3. D	1.10
4. G	1.10
5. A	1.19
6. H	1.19
7. B	1.11
8. F	1.11
9. B	1.2
10. J	1.2
11. B	1.2
12. H	1.2

13.   Answer: See discussion below.

Discussion

Tip: How can the size of the object help you decide if it would be a good unit of measure?

Have children

- point to each object and visualize measuring the length of a bus with that object.

- tell if it would take many units or few units to measure.

- tell how accurate a measurement they think they would get.

Accept all reasonable answers. Some children may suggest the baseball bat. As this is the largest object, it would most quickly measure the bus.

Some children may say that the whistle and paper clip are smaller, so they would give a more accurate measurement.

Then ask children to describe another strategy they could use to solve the problem.

1.11 Selects appropriate instrument for determining specified measurement of height, weight, capacity, and temperature.

14.   Answer: The child selects two items of different lengths and describes how they start in the same place, but the shorter item ends before the longer item.

Discussion

Tip: What can you do to compare the length of two objects?

Have children

- select two objects.

- hold or place them next to one another to align them on one side.

- see if they are aligned on both sides or just one.

Then ask children to describe the items that are different lengths. Encourage discussion that includes the words "same length," "longer," and "shorter."

1.9 Identifies relationships (larger than, largest, smaller than, smallest, same size as, same shape as, inside, outside, on, left, and right).

1.19 Compares weight of two real objects (heavier than, lighter than) and capacity of two real containers (more than, less than) using both dry and liquid measure units, and compares the height of two real objects (shorter than, taller than).

15. **Answer: Accept all reasonable answers.**

    Possible answers may include:

    Longer than my arm: book shelf, teacher's desk, chalkboard

    Shorter than my arm: crayon, book, eraser

Discussion

Tip: How can you use a string to compare the length of objects?

Have children

- work with a partner to cut strings that measure the length of their arms.

- compare the length of the string with objects in the classroom.

- draw pictures to show which objects were longer and shorter than their arms.

Then ask children to describe how they determined which objects were longer and shorter than their arms.

1.9 Identifies relationships (larger than, largest, smaller than, smallest, same size as, same shape as, inside, outside, on, left, and right).

1.19 Compares weight of two real objects (heavier than, lighter than) and capacity of two real containers (more than, less than) using both dry and liquid measure units, and compares the height of two real objects (shorter than, taller than).

16. **Answer: Accept all reasonable answers that describe measuring length (or height) of objects such as: pencil, book, paintbrush, string. Children should say they line up the left-hand edge of the ruler with the left side of the object so that the beginning of the object is at the beginning of the ruler. Then they look at the other end of the object and match it to the number on the ruler.**

Discussion

Tip: What measuring tool can you use to find out how long things are?

Have children name things that can be measured in inches or centimeters.

Then ask children to describe how to use a ruler to measure length.

Encourage discussion that includes the words "longer," "shorter," "inch," and "centimeter."

1.10 Describes, orders, and measures length using inches and centimeters.

© Harcourt

17. **Answer: The crayon is about 9 centimeters long. Measurements will vary using paper clips. Each paper clip is longer than a centimeter, so it will take fewer paper clips to measure the same length.**

Discussion

Tip: How can you tell how long the crayon is?

Have children

- get a crayon and trace the length with a finger.
- make and place a paper clip chain edge to edge across the length of the crayon.
- count how many paper clips long the crayon is.
- measure the length with a centimeter ruler.
- compare.

Then ask children to tell how measuring in centimeters is different from measuring with paper clips.

Encourage discussion that compares a centimeter as a uniform unit of measure to a paper clip that can be different lengths.

1.1 Explores estimation of quantities of less than 100.

1.10 Describes, orders, and measures length using inches and centimeters.

18. **Answer: The airplane is heavier. It balances three cubes. The box is lighter. It balances two cubes.**

Discussion

Tip: How can you use the pan balance and cubes to find out which container is heavier?

Have children

- select two objects.
- place one object on one side of the pan balance and count and place cubes on the other side to balance it.
- repeat with the other object.
- compare the number of cubes used to balance each object.

Then ask children to explain the problem in their own words.

1.19 Compares weight of two real objects (heavier than, lighter than) and capacity of two real containers (more than, less than) using both dry and liquid measure units, and compares the height of two real objects (shorter than, taller than).

19. Answer: The jar holds more; the measuring cup holds less.

Discussion

Tip: How can you compare the contents of each container to find out which holds more and which holds less?

Have children

- select the container they think holds less.

- fill the container with water, sand, rice, or another item that pours.

- pour the contents of the container into the other container.

Then ask children to describe another way they could have solved the problem. Another solution would be for the child to scoop an item that pours into both containers and count how many scoops it takes to fill each one.

1.19 Compares weight of two real objects (heavier than, lighter than) and capacity of two real containers (more than, less than) using both dry and liquid measure units, and compares the height of two real objects (shorter than, taller than).

20. Answer: Children should explain that shapes showing fourths all show 4 equal parts.

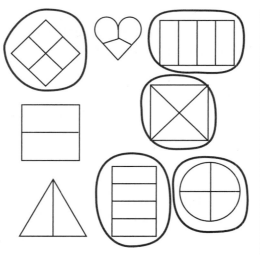

Discussion

Tip: If something is divided into fourths, how many equal parts are there?

Have children

- point to each shape and tell how many parts are shown.

- tell if the parts are equal.

Then ask children to tell what math words they need to know to solve the problem. Encourage discussion that includes the words "four" and "equal parts."

1.2 Recognizes different ways of representing fractions using concrete and pictorial models and words for one-half and one-fourth.

© Harcourt

Georgia Quality Core Curriculum Objectives

1.9 Identifies relationships (larger than, largest, smaller than, smallest, same size as, same shape as, inside, outside, on, left, and right).

.1.20 Selects the numeral that names a group of objects and matches a group of objects with the appropriate numeral for a given set containing 0 through 100 objects.

1.29 Selects elements (concrete objects) belonging to or not belonging to a given set.

1.33 Organizes elements of sets according to characteristics such as use, size, and shape.

1.34 Interprets data by reading bar graphs and pictographs using whole unit data.

1.36 Solves one- and two-step word problems related to appropriate first-grade objectives. Includes oral and written problems and problems with extraneous information, as well as information from sources such as bar graphs and pictographs.

1.44 Relates addition and subtraction to words, pictures, and concrete models, particularly sums and differences to 18 and related differences, and multiples of ten.

Item Numbers	Georgia QCC Objectives
1. A	1.9, 1.33
2. J	1.20, 1.29, 1.36
3. C	1.34, 1.36
4. F	1.34, 1.36
5. C	1.34, 1.36
6. H	
7. A	1.34
8. J	1.34, 1.36
9. B	1.34, 1.36
10. G	1.34, 1.36, 1.44
11. C	1.34, 1.36, 1.44
12. J	1.34, 1.36, 1.44

13. **Answer: Possible answers: tally marks for 5 squares and 5 triangles, or 6 large shapes and 4 small shapes**

1.33 Organizes elements of sets according to characteristics such as use, size, and shape.

Discussion

Tip: How can you make a table to present information about the shapes pictured?

Have children

- sort the shapes.
- draw the sorted shapes for each category.
- make tally marks in each category and total the tallies.

Then ask children to use the words "more," "fewer," and "how many."

14. **Answer: Baseball**

1.34 Interprets data by reading bar graphs and pictographs using whole unit data.

Discussion

Tip: How can counting help you solve the problem?

Children can count the number of pictures in each row. Then they can tell which number is the largest. That tells which sport most children like best.

15. **Answer: the child in the bathroom. See also discussion below.**

Discussion

Tip: What do you know about monkeys that might help you answer the question? How can you decide what to draw?

Have children

- talk about places where you usually see monkeys. Children might talk about the zoo or the rain forest.
- close their eyes and remember some things they see and do not see at home.

Then ask children to explain why their "unlikely" drawing is unlikely. Can they use the "What do you know about ____" question to check that one drawing is unlikely? Encourage discussion about things that are certain and impossible.

16.   Answer: Answers will vary.

Discussion

Tip: How many darks and lights showed up when the pointer was spun 10 times? What parts of the spinner are light and dark?

Children can tell how many of each were spun by looking at the tallies on the chart. They can see there are six light and four dark. If they look at the spinner, they will see there is more light area than dark. These two clues can give them an idea. They might predict more lights than darks. In 20 spins, they might predict 12 light and 8 dark. Reasonable answers will vary.

17.   Answer: 2

Discussion

Tip: How many of each number are on the spinner?

Have children note the number of times each number—1, 2, and 3—appears on the spinner. Children should conclude that there is one 1, two 2s, and one 3. Because there are more 2s than any other number, the pointer is most likely to land on 2.

18.   Answer: Accept all reasonable responses. For example, the child might say the graph shows the most coins chosen were dimes.

Discussion

Tip: If you pick more nickels than dimes, what will your graph look like?

Have children

- color a box in the "pennies" row for each penny.

- do the same for the nickels and dimes.

- compare the rows and describe what the graph shows.

Then ask children to make up a question and answer about their graph. Encourage discussion that includes "more," "fewer," "most," "fewest," and "in all."

19. Accept all reasonable answers.

1.34 Interprets data by reading bar graphs and pictographs using whole unit data.

Discussion

Tip: How can the results of a small survey help you predict the results of a larger survey?

Have children

- read the graph and tell which season the most children liked. They might note that summer had the most votes. Fall had the fewest votes.

- tell how the graph might change if more children were surveyed. They should predict that more squares will be filled in the graph. They also might predict that more children will say "summer" than "fall."

You might try a class survey and make a graph showing the results.

20. Answer: See graph.

1.34 Interprets data by reading bar graphs and pictographs using whole unit data.

Discussion

Tip: How can counting help you solve the problem?

Have children count the number of tallies in each section of the tally chart. Then they will color a square in the blank bar graph for each tally mark: four orange, six grape, and ten apple.

Georgia Quality Core Curriculum Objectives

1.37 Adds three 1-digit whole numbers presented vertically and horizontally (rewrite vertically) without regrouping.

1.38 Recalls addition facts (sums to 18) and related subtraction facts presented vertically and horizontally (rewrite vertically).

1.44 Relates addition and subtraction to words, pictures, and concrete models, particularly sums and differences to 18 and related differences, and multiples of ten.

1.45 Determines addition and subtraction facts up to 18 using strategies such as counting all of a set, part-whole, counting on, counting back, counting up, doubles, property of zero, and commutativity of addition.

Item Numbers	Georgia QCC Objectives
1. C	1.45
2. G	1.45
3. D	1.45
4. F	1.45
5. B	1.44, 1.45
6. H	1.38, 1.45
7. D	1.45
8. G	1.45
9. C	1.37, 1.45
10. F	1.37, 1.45
11. D	1.38
12. J	1.38

13.   Answer: 7 + 6 = 13 or 6 + 7 = 13

Discussion

Tip: What does the story ask you to find out?

Have children identify what they are asked to find out. Then they can write down the number of red apples and the number of yellow apples and decide whether to add or subtract. Children can then write a number sentence and add 7 and 6 to solve the problem.

Have children summarize the process.

What did you do first?

How did you solve the problem?

How did you know whether to add or subtract?

14.   Answer: 10; 5 + 4 = 9 or 4 + 5 = 9

Discussion

Tip: How are the two number sentences different?

The first number sentence is a double. The second number sentence is a doubles-minus-one fact. The sum of the second fact is one less than the sum of the first fact.

15.   Answer: 14 – 7 = 7; Sam has 7 more airplanes.

Discussion

Tip: How can knowing about doubles help you write a number sentence?

Since children are comparing and finding the difference, they need to subtract.

They know that 7 + 7 = 14, so 14 – 7 = 7.

16. Answer: Accept all reasonable answers that describe finding a sum of 16. For example: 9 + 1 + 6.

Discussion

Tip: How do you add two numbers by using the make-a-ten strategy?

Have children

- name the numbers they are being asked to add.
- tell which is the greater number.
- draw that many counters.
- draw counters from the lesser number to fill the ten-frame.
- draw the extra counters to ten to find the sum.

Then ask children to tell how they solved the problem in their own words.

1.45 Determines addition and subtraction facts up to 18 using strategies such as counting all of a set, part-whole, counting on, counting back, counting up, doubles, property of zero, and commutativity of addition.

17. Answer: 6 children

Discussion

Tip: How can you act out the story to help solve this problem?

You can have 6 children pretend to be in a lunch line. Then you can have 2 children get out of the line. Then you can have 2 new children get in the line. What can you tell about the number of children who get in and get out of the line? Does that change the number of children who are in the line to start? Why or why not? Children should realize that the original number of children, 6, are still in the lunch line. If two children get out of the line and two more children get in, the original number of children does not change.

1.41 Uses appropriate mathematical symbols (+, –, =).

1.44 Relates addition and subtraction to words, pictures, and concrete models, particularly sums and differences to 18 and related differences, and multiples of ten.

1.45 Determines addition and subtraction facts up to 18 using strategies such as counting all of a set, part-whole, counting on, counting back, counting up, doubles, property of zero, and commutativity of addition.

18. Answer: 4 + ___ = 12, 8 crayons

Discussion

Tip: How can drawing a picture help you solve the problem?

Children can draw 4 crayons. They can draw 12 crayons. Then they can count the difference and write a number sentence: 4 + ___ = 12.

1.44 Relates addition and subtraction to words, pictures, and concrete models, particularly sums and differences to 18 and related differences, and multiples of ten.

1.45 Determines addition and subtraction facts up to 18 using strategies such as counting all of a set, part-whole, counting on, counting back, counting up, doubles, property of zero, and commutativity of addition.

19. Answer: 6

Discussion

Tip: How can connecting cubes help you solve this problem?

Children can connect 5 cubes. Then they can connect more cubes until they have 11. Then they can count up from 5 until they reach 11. That will tell them the missing number.

1.38 Recalls addition facts (sums to 18) and related subtraction facts presented vertically and horizontally (rewrite vertically).

1.45 Determines addition and subtraction facts up to 18 using strategies such as counting all of a set, part-whole, counting on, counting back, counting up, doubles, property of zero, and commutativity of addition.

20. Answer: 7

Discussion

Tip: How can drawing a picture help you solve the problem?

Children can draw 9 objects, for example, circles. Then they can draw more circles until they have 16. Then they can count up from 9 until they reach 16. That will tell them the number of missing circles.

1.38 Recalls addition facts (sums to 18) and related subtraction facts presented vertically and horizontally (rewrite vertically).

1.45 Determines addition and subtraction facts up to 18 using strategies such as counting all of a set, part-whole, counting on, counting back, counting up, doubles, property of zero, and commutativity of addition.

Georgia Quality Core Curriculum Objectives

1.1 Explores estimation of quantities of less than 100.

1.20 Selects the numeral that names a group of objects and matches a group of objects with the appropriate numeral for a given set containing 0 through 100 objects.

1.27 Identifies place value by determining number of tens and ones in a given number.

1.30 Recognizes equivalent and nonequivalent sets using one-to-one correspondence.

1.39 Uses models such as base ten blocks, pictorial representation, and number line to explore adding and subtracting two-digit numbers without regrouping.

1.40 Adds and subtracts 2-digit whole numbers without regrouping vertically and horizontally (rewrite vertically).

1.44 Relates addition and subtraction to words, pictures, and concrete models, particularly sums and differences to 18 and related differences, and multiples of ten.

1.45 Determines addition and subtraction facts up to 18 using strategies such as counting all of a set, part-whole, counting on, counting back, counting up, doubles, property of zero, and commutativity of addition.

Item Numbers	Georgia QCC Objectives
1. C	1.20, 1.45
2. G	1.20, 1.30
3. A	1.20, 1.30
4. G	1.20
5. D	1.30, 1.44, 1.45
6. J	1.44, 1.45
7. C	1.27, 1.39, 1.40
8. G	1.27, 1.39, 1.40
9. C	1.27, 1.39, 1.40
10. F	1.27, 1.39, 1.40
11. D	1.27, 1.39, 1.40
12. G	1.1, 1.44

13. Answer: 10 circles

Discussion

Tip: What are you asked to find out?

Children need to find out how many circles there are in all. After they draw two groups of five circles, they can count the circles, add the numbers in both groups (5 + 5), or count by fives (5, 10) to find the total.

1.20 Selects the numeral that names a group of objects and matches a group of objects with the appropriate numeral for a given set containing 0 through 100 objects.

1.45 Determines addition and subtraction facts up to 18 using strategies such as counting all of a set, part-whole, counting on, counting back, counting up, doubles, property of zero, and commutativity of addition.

14. Answer: 2 are in each group.

Discussion

Tip: What are you asked to find out?

Children need to find out how many circles are in each group. Perhaps the easiest way to start would be for them to draw one circle in each of five groups, then add one circle at a time to each group until they have drawn all ten circles.

1.20 Selects the numeral that names a group of objects and matches a group of objects with the appropriate numeral for a given set containing 0 through 100 objects.

1.45 Determines addition and subtraction facts up to 18 using strategies such as counting all of a set, part-whole, counting on, counting back, counting up, doubles, property of zero, and commutativity of addition.

15. Answer: 2 groups

Discussion

Tip: How is this problem different from Problem 14?

This problem has different numbers; it asks for the number of groups, instead of the number in each group. Children can draw groups of six until they have drawn 12 circles.

1.20 Selects the numeral that names a group of objects and matches a group of objects with the appropriate numeral for a given set containing 0 through 100 objects.

1.45 Determines addition and subtraction facts up to 18 using strategies such as counting all of a set, part-whole, counting on, counting back, counting up, doubles, property of zero, and commutativity of addition.

16. Answer: 3 stars in each group

Discussion

Tip: How can a picture help you solve the problem?

Children can show 5 groups of stars with 3 stars in each group because they have a total of 15 stars.

1.44 Relates addition and subtraction to words, pictures, and concrete models, particularly sums and differences to 18 and related differences, and multiples of ten.

17. Answer: 92 pennies

Discussion

Tip: How can a model help you solve the problem?

Children can make a model of tens and ones with base-ten blocks. They can show each number, 38 and 54. They can add the ones. Then they can see if you have to regroup. Then they can add the tens to get the total number of pennies.

1.44 Relates addition and subtraction to words, pictures, and concrete models, particularly sums and differences to 18 and related differences, and multiples of ten.

18. Answer: 9 ducks

Discussion

Tip: How can base-ten blocks help you solve the problem?

Children can use the blocks to show the tens and ones: 2 tens and 7 ones – 1 ten and 8 ones. They can see that you need to regroup. So now they have 17 ones – 8 ones, which is 9. Then they see that there are no tens. So the answer is 9.

1.22 Models and pictorially represents whole numbers through 100 using groups of tens and ones and orally names numbers (e.g., 3 tens, 2 ones; thirty-two; or 30 + 2 = 32).

1.27 Identifies place value by determining number of tens and ones in a given number.

1.44 Relates addition and subtraction to words, pictures, and concrete models, particularly sums and differences to 18 and related differences, and multiples of ten.

19. Answer: 45¢ + 24¢ = 69¢

Discussion

Tip: What does the box of crayons cost? What does the ruler cost? What do you have to find out?

Children have to find out how much money they need to buy the two items. They can add 45¢ and 24¢. Have children write a plus sign in the circle and then add the two amounts.

1.40 Adds and subtracts 2-digit whole numbers without regrouping vertically and horizontally (rewrite vertically).

1.41 Uses appropriate mathematical symbols (+, –, =).

1.44 Relates addition and subtraction to words, pictures, and concrete models, particularly sums and differences to 18 and related differences, and multiples of ten.

20. Answer: 20¢

Discussion

Tip: How much money do you have? How much does the goldfish cost? What do you have to find out?

Children have to find out how much money they will have after buying the goldfish. They can subtract 55¢ from 75¢.

1.40 Adds and subtracts 2-digit whole numbers without regrouping vertically and horizontally (rewrite vertically).

1.41 Uses appropriate mathematical symbols (+, –, =).

1.44 Relates addition and subtraction to words, pictures, and concrete models, particularly sums and differences to 18 and related differences, and multiples of ten.

© Harcourt